Feng Shui

From Beginner to Expert,
Illustrated Version

Start Using Feng Shui
Today to Attract
Happiness and Success

by Joline McMathews

Table of Contents

Introduction

Feng Shui is quickly gaining worldwide attention as a new method for achieving success at work, at home, and in every other aspect of people's lives. It has been proven to work effectively with people all around the world. Numerous testimonies attest to the fact that people's lives, in general, have improved, and they're reaping success in areas where they had failed dismally in the past. Also, Feng Shui has also brought peace and good health to those who practice it.

If you've labored all your life and remain unsuccessful; if you've tried all sorts of methods to attain success but nothing has worked, and you're about to throw in the towel - DON'T! Feng Shui might be the perfect tool to help you achieve your dreams. It can be the key that will unlock the door to your success. You just need to learn how it works, and then apply it properly into your life.

When you follow the instructions and believe in the power of Feng Shui, then there's no reason for it not to work for you as it has for so many others. Feng Shui will help you balance your existence and fill those empty voids with positive energy that can work harmoniously towards your success.

1

If you're ready to harmonize all the aspects of your life and achieve the success, you truly deserve, then read on to learn about enhancing the Feng Shui energy using the Bagua Map. Learn how to compute your Feng Shui lucky number and determine your most promising areas utilizing the Lo Shu square and other Feng Shui tools. Become one of those who have experienced the immense power of Feng Shui in their lives. Acquire the essential knowledge of how Feng Shui can harness the fields of energy at your home and at your workplace to transform your life forever. Let's get started!

Chapter 1: Feng Shui Basics and History

Feng Shui (pronounced as "Feng shoy" or "Fung Shway") is translated literally as "wind-water." It is strongly related to Daoism, a religious and philosophical Chinese tradition that maintains that one must live according to the cosmic order of the universe. It originated in China and was part of the Chinese tradition of geomancy, which initially pertained to the proper positioning of structures to harmonize the energy or Chi they produce in congruence with the environment or the forces existing in the universe. Nowadays, Feng Shui has been incorporated into furniture arrangements, room designs, and almost all types of structures that can be arranged.

What is Feng Shui?

Feng Shui is an ancient Chinese practice that emphasizes the belief that all things emit energy, or Chi, that can affect the course of other things around them. The basic elements, the wind, and water, are considered the most important of the five elements because the wind provides the air that we breathe, and water is an essential substance that our body needs. Without the wind we would die in minutes; without water, we would die in days. The combination of these two determines the climate in the region we live in, thereby determining what food we can get and how much food we can obtain. It operates on the idea that the Yin and Yang and the five elements should be balanced in the body to achieve health, happiness, and success.

The fact is that energy emanates from all things revolving around you. The energy is known as *Qi* or *Chi*. The literal meaning of *Chi* is breath or air. Of course, the philosophical or figurative sense is energy flow or life force. The concept of this power is not limited to just the Chinese culture. Chi has different names in various parts of the world: *lüng* in Tibetan culture, *prana* in Hinduism, *Manitou* in the American indigenous cultures, *ruah* in Jewish tradition, *mana* in the Hawaiian belief system and vital energy in Western philosophy.

For you to succeed and be happy and at peace, all of these energy fields must harmonize with one another. Imagine multiple people trying to move a desk, each pushing in a different direction. Are they going to get anywhere? No. It's the same with Feng Shui. For it to work, all of the energy forces in your life must be concentrated on a single area, making it more efficient and more robust. This area will attract positive energy ensuring your prosperity in love, work, health, and all aspects of your life.

Another name for Feng Shui is the art of placement. It follows the belief that how you place yourself, your furnishings and other possessions within your environs will determine the life experience you have. I allows you to bring accord, enjoyment, happiness um into your environment.

Feng Shui

is believed to have been practiced long the invention of the magnetic compass. rchaeologists have found that the Hongshan and Yangshao cultures have the earliest recorded indication of the use of Feng Shui. The Yangshao culture existed along the Yellow River between 5000 BC and 3000 BC. The Hongshan culture was present in the area between Liaoning in the south and Mongolia in the north, approximately between 4700 BC and 2900 BC. This fact indicates that the practice, or at least some form of it, was already being followed about five thousand to seven thousand years ago.

Since the magnetic compass came into existence three thousand five hundred years later, Feng Shui originally depended upon astronomy to determine the relationship between the universe and humans. Ruins excavated at Banpo in the Yellow River Valley were found to have their doors aligned with the appearance of the *Yingshi* asterism right after the winter solstice. An asterism means a group of stars that form a recognizable pattern, regardless of whether they belong to one constellation or more than one. These ruins have been dated to around 4000 BC. During the Zhou dynasty, capital cities were built once *Yingshi*, now known as *Ding, appeared in the sky*. Various excavations have yielded sites where buildings such as palaces were found to be standing along a north-south axis. Also, the excavations of other sites show signs of *gaitain* cosmography being used. *Gaitain* works on the principle that heaven is represented by round, while earth is represented by a square. Pretty much every capital city in China followed the rules laid out by Feng Shui regarding layouts and designs. This fact is especially evident in excavated sites that had grand structures, which were aligned according to the rules of Feng Shui regarding their arrangement and architectural plan. The rules were codified in the *Kaogong Ji* during the Zhou period. The carpenter's manual known as *Lu Ban Jing* covered the rules for builders.

The oldest instances of Feng Shui instruments are the *shi* or the *liuren* astrolabes. Archaeologists found them in tombs that dated back to a period between 278 BC and 209 BC. They have the same markings as those contained on a magnetic compass.

The magnetic compass was eventually devised to be used in Feng Shui. One of the traditional instruments of Feng Shui is the Luopan or the Chinese magnetic compass.

During the Cultural Revolution imposed by the Chinese government in the 1960s, the practice of Feng Shui was suppressed.

When to use Feng Shui

You can use Feng Shui in your office, or at home in each of your individual rooms, or at your home as a more holistic approach. You can use it anywhere that you're able to apply its concepts.

Your Feng Shui must be coupled with good intentions, kindness, the sincere desire to help, and a positive outlook on life. You can start using Feng

Shui by setting your goals first and then determining your Feng Shui using the Bagua Map. You have to identify specific goals that you wish to achieve so that you'll know what to focus on.

Chapter 2: Important Theories and Schools of Thought

Theories behind Feng Shui

There are fundamental underlying principles that are utilized in Feng Shui. These have to do with *chi*, polarity, and the *Bagua*.

Chi or *Qi* is energy that moves and can be positive and negative. When related to Feng Shui *Chi* is involved in the orientation of a building, how old it is and how it has interacted with the environment around it. As per the Book of Burial, burial was meant to take advantage of vital *qi* or congealed *qi*, the energy that gives rise to life. As such, Feng Shui was crucial in the arrangement of graves, burial sites, and other structures. People who wanted to weaken their enemies would destroy the enemies' graveyards to weaken the enemies' *qi*. Loupans are used to detect the flow of *chi*, although that is not their only use.

The *Yin* and *Yang* are used to express polarity, which therefore becomes similar to a magnetic dipole. In other words, polarity has two parts: one that pushes and one that pulls. There are also the five elements, namely earth, metal, wood, fire, and water. These don't actually represent the substances so much as they do the elements or forces of life. When the two forces cancel each other out, the balance obtained is what Earth is. Feng Shui aims to align buildings, sites, objects and even cities within the *yin* and *yang* force fields.

The *Bagua* (eight trigrams) are two diagrams that are fundamental to Feng Shui. The first one to be developed was the *Lo,* or, River *Chart*, also known as *Luoshu.* The arrangement of the Bagua referred to as the Later Heaven arrangement is now and again associated with this. The *Yellow River Chart* came later and is sometimes linked to the Earlier Heaven arrangement. The two charts are related to the Turtle calendar from the Yao period, which was dated to around 2300 BC and to celestial events that took place around the sixth millennium BC. The two diagrams are also connected with the *sifang* or the four directions method of divination that was in use during the Shang dynasty.

Two general types of Feng Shui schools of thought:

1. **Form** – This is the oldest school of Feng Shui. It is described in the Book of the Tomb,

16

and a complete presentment can be found in the Book of Burial. It was first used to determine the location and direction of tombs and was later applied in the layouts of other buildings such as palaces and homes. The word 'form' is used with reference to the environs of the building in question – rivers, plateaus, mountains, other buildings and many other such factors. It also takes into account the five celestial animals which are the green dragon, phoenix, white tiger, yellow snake and black turtle. These are considered along with the *yin* and *yang* and the five traditional elements of earth, metal, wood, fire, and water. It works by analyzing the flow of the wind and the water and the shape of the land to determine a location that has the ideal *qi*. Also considered are circumstances such as the assembly of the building and the birth of the occupants. This type uses the Feng Shui Bagua Map in determining your best Feng Shui arrangement. It is composed of 9 small squares that you need to overlay onto the floor plan of your space.

2. **Compass** – This school is more recent compared to the Form School and is based on the eight cardinal directions. Adherents of this school believe that each direction has unique *qi*. This type uses a compass and astrological

tools to determine your Feng Shui. The compass used is the Luopan, which is a disc that has formulae marked in concentric rings around the magnetic compass. The Compass School uses two techniques known as the Flying Star and the Eight Mansions.

The Flying Star technique combines the various principles of Feng Shui such as *yin-yang*, the exchanges of the five elements, the Lo Shu numbers, the eight trigrams and the 24 Space Mountains. It creates an astrological chart by using time, space and objects to analyze the positive and negative auras of an edifice.

The Eight Mansions technique is also known as the Eight House Feng Shui. It uses complicated formulae to determine the *sha qi* or dangerous energy flow in any direction. Based on the house trigram, it also figures out poor land formation. The house is divided into nine palaces, eight of which are aligned to the eight cardinal directions and one of which is in the center. It also involves the calculation of your Life Gua number according to which year you were born in, to determine which four directions are propitious for you and which are not.

This technique is readily applicable to completed homes or buildings but is not convenient to use for individual rooms. It has eight sections, with one center space.

There is no clear indication as to which school is superior. Most modern practitioners borrow heavily from both schools.

Western Feng Shui schools of thought

Most of the western schools try to abridge and clarify the principles of Feng Shui that are prevalent in the two traditional schools. These schools tend to use the Bagua more than any other Feng Shui tool.

1. **Aspirations Method** – The Aspirations Method is also known as the Eight Life Aspirations school of Feng Shui. It connects each of the eight cardinal directions with a particular life ambition or desire such as love, fame, family, wealth and so on. These come from the Bagua system of eight aspirations. However, this is the only way in which the method utilizes geomancy.

2. **Black Sect** – In the 1970s, Thomas Lin Yun introduced this method to the United States of America. Its correct name is Black Sect Tantric Buddhism Feng Shui. It doesn't just embrace the principles of Feng Shui but also incorporates various philosophies from Taoism, Tibetan Buddhism, and transcendentalism. This school focuses on the interiors rather than the exterior of a building. The Bagua is oriented to the entrance instead of the compass. As always, the eight sectors represent different parts of your life.

Chapter 3:   The Five Elements of Feng Shui

The Five Elements are used to describe the shapes, colors and materials that surround you and the attributes they bring to your life. For you to succeed with Feng Shui, the five elements: water, fire, wood, earth, and metal, have to be in harmony with one another. Each element has specific shapes and colors and represents specific aspects of your life.

- *Water* – Water brings relaxation and somewhat contradictorily movement and flow into your life. Its power is gentle, similar to that of a meandering river. It signifies creativity and insight. The objects associated with this element are fish bowls, aquariums, and even fountains. The element itself is represented by mirrors and glass. The shape of the element itself is not rigid but something that swirls or curves. Even objects contain this form such as rugs, curtains, and even items such as slip covers represent the element. The colors that represent the Water element are black and deep blues, the colors of deep water.

- *Fire* – If Water is the element of relaxation, Fire is almost the exact opposite. It brings emotion, passion, and high energy. It signifies visibility and the high energy characteristic. Objects associated with the Fire element are characteristically hot such as a blazing fireplace or burning candles. The shape of the element is a triangle, meant to represent a flame. The colors associated with the element are passionate like the element itself: pink, red, crimson, scarlet, orange and dark purple.

- *Wood* – The Wood element brings in vitality, expansion, and growth in your life. It signifies cooperation, new beginnings, and self-growth. The Wood element objects are also wooden such as furniture, plants, flowers, doors and picture frames. The shape of the element is rectangular, and the colors associated with the element are green, and teal meant to represent leaves from trees.

- *Earth* – The Earth element brings grounding, balance, and stability into your life. It signifies control, nourishment, and balance. The objects of this element are generally made of earth such as the marble or granite countertops in your kitchen, the tile floors in your house and any clay pots or accessories in your home. The Earth element's shape is square, and the colors are the colors of the earth: brown like the land, yellow like the sun and terracotta like clay.

- *Metal* – Metal is strong, and so the Metal element brings clarity and strength into your life. It signifies calmness, ingenuity, and excellent planning. Metal element objects can range from wrought iron furniture to metal headboards or even light fixtures. Even electronics and computers are considered Metal objects as is fluorescent light. Metal is represented by the round shape of a metal coin, and its colors are also metallic such as gold and silver. Pastels and white and grey are also considered Metal colors.

You need to use the Five Elements in your surroundings to bring the powers related to the metals into your life. A roaring fireplace will bring in the Fire element, which means an aura of energy. Adding an indoor green plant will help you with blocked creativity since the object is associated with wood. If it isn't possible to associate the objects with the various elements, you can use the shapes and colors associated with them to be able to enjoy those properties. However, you will get the most power and achieve the best results if you combine the object, the shape, and the element. All five elements are vital to good Feng Shui.

Chapter 4: Learning to Use the Feng Shui Bagua Map

To use Feng Shui successfully, you have to use your Bagua Map as a tool. The Bagua Map is an energy map or grid that contains the areas that correspond to the various aspects of your life. Bagua literally means "8 areas." Your Bagua Map will serve as your guide in determining the type of energy present in specific areas of your house or room. You can refer to the following guidelines to use your Feng Shui Bagua Map.

Step #1 – Have a positive frame of mind

While enhancing your Feng Shui areas, you must strive to be optimistic at all times. This attitude helps a lot in attracting more positive energy from external energy sources. Moreover, being positive will exude your own positive energy, increasing your Chi (total energy) and maintaining the balance of your Yin and Yang. These are crucial aspects to observe for good Feng Shui to occur.

Step 2 – De-clutter your area

You have to empty the space and de-clutter it first. A clean, well-ventilated, and well-lighted area will be much easier to enhance using good Feng Shui. Such an area will prevent negative energy from staying behind and occupying that particular space. Removing clutter will also provide an space for your Feng Shui arrangement later.

Step #3 – Choose your three most important goals

Determine your three most important goals in life and chart your Feng Shui using the map. Focusing on specific goals will increase your chances of implementing good Feng Shui successfully. Develop your home as a powerful Feng Shui tool for your success.

Step #4 – Align your home's entry point to the bottom of the Bagua Map

Align your home's entry point to the lower portion of the Feng Shui Bagua Map. The particular example presented in this book is a map for your home.

Step #5 – Read clockwise starting from the left center section

Go over the map by reading clockwise starting from the left center section. Take note of the categories indicated on each of the sections. If you have selected your three goals, identify which grid they correspond to on the Feng Shui Bagua Map presented on the next page.

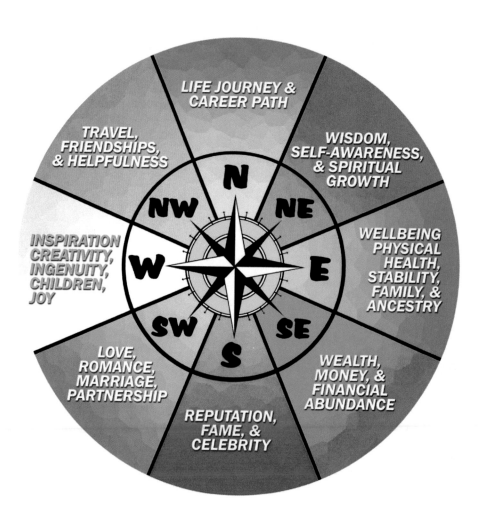

LIFE JOURNEY &
CAREER PATH

TRAVEL,
FRIENDSHIPS,
& HELPFULNESS

WISDOM,
SELF-AWARENESS,
& SPIRITUAL
GROWTH

INSPIRATION
CREATIVITY,
INGENUITY,
CHILDREN,
JOY

WELLBEING
PHYSICAL
HEALTH,
STABILITY,
FAMILY, &
ANCESTRY

LOVE,
ROMANCE,
MARRIAGE,
PARTNERSHIP

WEALTH,
MONEY, &
FINANCIAL
ABUNDANCE

REPUTATION,
FAME, &
CELEBRITY

N NE E SE S SW W NW

The compass Bagua Map on the left is most commonly applicable when creating an overall sense of Feng Shui throughout your home, or any other building or structure, and you can do so through the use of a compass. Just align the compass with true North, and you'll be able to identify what areas correspond to particular Feng Shui categories.

On the other hand, the form map on the next page is utilized more frequently for homes, using the map itself, since that's easier than using a compass for some. In this case, just overlay the grid onto the floor plan of your house, aligning the bottom of the grid with the entry wall (the wall where the front door is), and work around the house from there.

In any case, it's perfectly acceptable to use either map, choosing the one that is most applicable to your own needs.

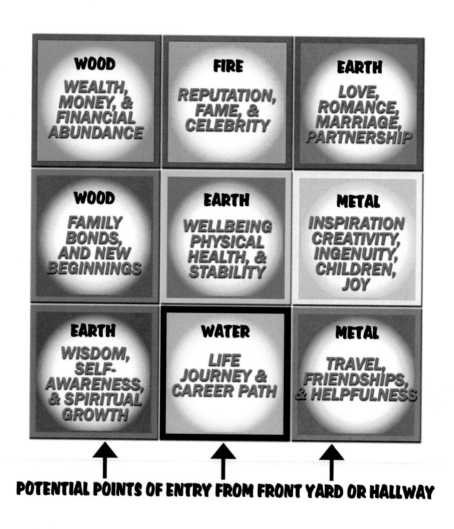

WOOD	FIRE	EARTH
WEALTH, MONEY, & FINANCIAL ABUNDANCE	REPUTATION, FAME, & CELEBRITY	LOVE, ROMANCE, MARRIAGE, PARTNERSHIP
WOOD	EARTH	METAL
FAMILY BONDS, AND NEW BEGINNINGS	WELLBEING PHYSICAL HEALTH, & STABILITY	INSPIRATION CREATIVITY, INGENUITY, CHILDREN, JOY
EARTH	WATER	METAL
WISDOM, SELF-AWARENESS, & SPIRITUAL GROWTH	LIFE JOURNEY & CAREER PATH	TRAVEL, FRIENDSHIPS, & HELPFULNESS

POTENTIAL POINTS OF ENTRY FROM FRONT YARD OR HALLWAY

Step #6 – Enhance the goal you have selected by using these tools

You have to utilize the following enhancement tools to increase your chances of success. Before you enrich these areas, though, you have to de-clutter them. Remove all unnecessary items that don't contribute to good Feng Shui. Here are methods of enhancing each grid or aspect in your Bagua Map.

- *Family, Ancestry, Bonds, and New Beginnings (East)* – As shown in the map, the preferred material is wood, and the color must be blue, green, yellow, and natural browns. You can enhance this by displaying family pictures, green items or prints, wooden materials and items that can be displayed vertically. Take note, though, if this area happens to correspond with the location of your bedroom then family pictures shouldn't be shown in your bedroom.

- *Money, Wealth, and Financial Abundance (Southeast)* – The involved element is wood. You can use the recommended colors instead, which are green, gold, and purple. Display items that symbolize wealth and prosperity.

Displaying materials that express your gratitude for the blessings you have received are also good Feng Shui enhancements.

- *Reputation, Fame, and Celebrity (South)* – Since you can't always utilize the fire element to reconstruct this space or area, you'll have to rely on lighting items, such as candles or materials that create light. You can use animal pictures and triangular-shaped objects as wall decors. Leather items enhance good Feng Shui too. The recommended colors for this area are red and orange-red.

- *Love, Romance, Marriage, and Partnership (Southwest)* – The element involved is earth. You can display items that evoke love and closeness such as couple's hand-bands, or hats. The preferred color is pink.

- *Inspiration, Creativity, Ingenuity, Children, and Joy (West)* – The element involved is metal. You can enhance this aspect in your life by using oval or rounded materials. It's best if these are made of metal. Display items that represent the future such as goal maps or plans. The best color for this area is white or light colors.

- *Travel, Friendships, Helpfulness, and Blessings (Northwest)* – The element involved is metal, but the recommended color is white or grey. You can display your travel photos and the pictures of people you have helped or plan to support. You can also hang pictures of places you want to visit in the future or people you want to help.

- *Life Journey and Career Path (North)* – The element water belongs to this area. You can display pictures of bodies of water, or paintings of water. Mirrors and glasses are excellent display items in this area. Use materials that are colored black or any dark shade.

- *Wisdom, Self-Awareness, and Spiritual Growth (Northeast)* – Earth is the element indicated in this area. Create a study area where you can display books, a small blackboard, and other materials for studying. Use the colors green and blue or shades of these two colors to enhance this particular area of your life. A captivating view of the mountains and the sea are superb images for this area.

- *Wellbeing, Physical Health, Unity, Balance, and Stability (Center)* – The element is the same as knowledge, and the colors recommended are earth colors such as yellow and brown. You can display square items and objects made up of earth. However, don't crowd the areas. This area is the heart of the Bagua Map so most of the area must be clear to allow the free flow of energy from the other grids to the center. In the compass map, the center space is empty.

Step #7 – Enhance the Feng Shui energy on three aspects of your life that you've selected

It's wise to focus first on the three goals/areas or issues you've previously selected. It may seem easy enhancing all of the areas simultaneously, but it's difficult. Improve the three areas first before proceeding to the rest. Little by little does it. Haphazardly accomplishing things will result in haphazard results. Turn the energy forces from these three areas to provide you a means to control where you would want to go.

Re-design and re-arrange these areas according to the Feng Shui recommendations to allow the energy forces to harmonize with each other into one tremendous power to boost your success.

Step #8 - Shift to other areas of your life, after succeeding with your first three goals

After you've succeeded in enhancing the first three areas you've chosen, you can move to another three areas. Strengthen these areas the same way you did the first three. Nevertheless, be aware that your effort must be coupled with good intentions. Karma's role in good Feng Shui should never be discounted. No matter how you enhance these areas using the Bagua Map, if you have bad will and intent towards other people, you will never succeed. Good intentions and motivations contribute towards the accomplishment of your goals, so be good to people.

Step #9 – Assume the command position

In organizing and enhancing your areas or spaces, always take the command position. This is a space where you can sit or lie down comfortably while being aware of everything that's happening inside the area. An example is arranging your study table in such a way that you can see anyone who enters your room even while reading or studying.

You can also use the Kua numbers to determine which direction you should be facing. Designated directions according to your personal Kua number can be found in Chapter 7.

Step #10 – Maintain and keep strengthening your Bagua areas

It's now up to you to maintain or strengthen all the areas in your Feng Shui Bagua Map. If there are areas that are not mentioned, you'll have to classify them based on the 9 major grids in your Bagua Map.

These are the steps that you have to use in order to promote Feng Shui in your life and career. You can modify according to your convenience but make sure you've accomplished the first two steps firsts. Implement the usage of the map properly and you'll surely achieve success.

These are the general steps to follow overall when you are using the Bagua Map. Now, you need to know exactly how to use the Bagua Map for your home.

1. **Design Your Floor Plan**

To begin the process of aligning your home or office with the Feng Shui Bagua Map, you need to make a drawing of the floor plan of your house. Mark the position of the front door. This position determines the direction of the placement of the Bagua Map through your floor plan.

This floor plan will include everything that is under your roof or is a part of the foundation. This could include a garage, a patio, a porch or anything else that may be attached to your home.

Make sure that you draw the appropriate shape. The shapes you'll commonly come across are rectangular, round and square. In addition, there are also L-shaped, Z-shaped, U-shaped or T-shaped homes. You may also find some homes built in the shape of a pyramid, although this is rather rare.

When drawing your floor plan, include any portions that jut out such as bay windows or any other architectural features.

If you live in a home with more than one story, you need to draw a separate floor plan for each. If the basement and attic are proper rooms, and in use, they need to be included in the plans. If, however, they are merely crawl spaces, then you don't need to include them. Even a full-size basement or attic that is not being used need not be included in the plans.

Don't Feng Shui all the floors together. Finish with one floor and then move on to the next, till you've done the entire house.

The first floor is the most important since this is typically where the highest amount of activity occurs. It is also where the *qi/chi* energy enters the dwelling via the front door. It then meanders throughout the rest of the home. So, focus on the first floor first.

2. Draw the Bagua Map

The paper you use to make the Bagua Map should be of the same size as that of the floor plan. Similarly, the Bagua Map must be the same size as the dimensions of the floor. Depending upon the shape of your floor plan, draw a rectangular or square map.

The actual Bagua Map is octagonal - it has eight sides. This octagon can be converted into a rectangle or a square since these are easiest to work with. If your home is circular, then draw an octagonal map.

Based on the Feng Shui maps divide the shape into nine squares. A home that is square or rectangular is easiest to work with because it won't have any missing corners. But many homes are not perfectly rectangular or square and have missing corners that must be dealt with.

Now you must determine where to place the front door when the floor plan is placed over the Feng Shui Bagua Map.

3. **Decide the orientation of the front door or entrance**

You can use two ways of determining how the front door needs to be aligned. The proper alignment of the front door is very important because that is where the '*chi*' enters the he building from.

The first method is the compass method. In this methodology you need to use a compass to determine what direction your front door faces. Based upon the coordinates you note down, you will need to place the floor plan so that it aligns with the corresponding directions in the Bagua Map.

The second method has many names. It is called the Black Hat or Western or BTB. This is a more modern method. You don't need a compass for the Western Method.

a) Compass Method

Use an ordinary or basic compass to determine what direction your front door faces. In the absence of a compass, you can use your smartphone or iPhone compass.

Compasses are sensitive to metal, and you won't get an accurate reading if you are near metal. Remove any metal, such bangles, bracelets or watches. Common sense dictates that standing near a car while using your compass isn't going to give you accurate readings. Metal is present in the walls of many homes and also in the door frame. Because of this you must not stand in the door frame. Instead stand inside the home and face the front door, or stand outside the house facing away from the front door.

If you feel that the readings you're getting are false because of metal in the door frame, try moving to different distances from the door while taking the readings. The optimum distance is three feet. However, if you're not sure, look for the point where the coordinates stop changing and become constant.

To get an accurate reading, note down the different coordinates, add them and divide the result by the number of readings.

Once you have the coordinates, match them to the coordinates in the map provided on the right.

COMPASS METHOD

Southeast 112.5° to 157.5°	South 157.5° to 202.5°	Southwest 202.5° to 247.5°
East 67.5° to 112.5°	Center	West 247.5° to 292.5°
Northeast 22.5° to 67.5°	North 337.5° to 22.5°	Northwest 292.5° to 337.5°

Once the coordinates have been matched, you will know where to place the front door while superimposing the Bagua Map over the floor plan.

For instance, if the coordinate you eventually arrive at is 57 degrees, the front door needs to be aligned with the northeast section of the map because the range in that section is 22.5 to 67.5 degrees and your coordinate falls within that range.

Therefore, in this example your front door aligns with the north-east section.

b) Western Method

In the Western method, you need to align your front door along the bottom of the Bagua Map.

If the door is in the left of the building, it should align with the Knowledge and Wisdom section of the map. If door is in the center of the building, then it needs to be aligned with the Career and Life Journey section. If the door is on the right hand side of the building it will align with the Helpful People and Travel section.

Different Home Shapes

These are the instructions to follow if your home is regularly shaped in an easy shape such as a square or rectangle. However, not all homes are so convenient and many homes come in shapes that might be difficult to apply the Feng Shui Bagua Map to. Homes that are L-shaped, T-shaped, Z-shaped, U-shaped and even pyramid-like or triangular in construction present difficulties when applying the Bagua Map. Because of their irregular shapes there can be missing corners that make it difficult for you to apply the Feng Shui Bagua Map. To deal with these difficulties here are descriptions of the various house shapes, both regular and irregular.

Square Shape – Square is the most perfect Feng Shui house shape. It is free of missing corners and is balanced since it is equal on all four sides. To align a house of this shape, your Bagua map sketch should also be square.

Rectangle Shape – A rectangle home that is not too narrow is also a good shape as far as Feng Shui is concerned. You just need to make your Bagua Map rectangular. However, if your home has a long and straight hallway, the '*chi*' energy could move too fast through it. The next shape tells you how to deal with it.

Rectangle Shape Narrow – As mentioned earlier, a rectangular shape that is too narrow can make the '*chi*' flow too fast through the house. This creates sharp *yang* energy which is very harsh. It is better that '*chi*' meanders through your home rather than rushing

49

through it. To break up the fast flow of the energy, put something in the hallway that makes the energy slow down and meander. You can use a plant or something else that helps to break up the straight line that the energy follows. The '*chi*' will then have to flow around the obstruction, thus slowing it down. However, if the hallway is to narrow to allow you to place something on the floor, you can hang a wind chime or something that dangles from the roof. Overall, though, this plan, too, is easy to use with a Bagua Map.

Circular Shape – Make an octagon Bagua Map sketch to superimpose on your floor plan sketch. Since we're essentially talking about a circle here, corners, missing or projecting won't be a problem. The energy flow in the house will go round creating more energy. Such a shape will work well for a commercial business such as a sports complex where lots of energy is desirable. A circular shaped home might have too much energy for some people to find it comfortable to live in.

Pyramid Shape – A church is more likely to be pyramid-shaped than a house. However, you do find some homes that are constructed in this shape. As mentioned in the colors and shapes section, a triangle represents the Fire element. As such, the shape is better suited to a building such as a church rather

50

than a home because the upper part of the building is then open in the manner of a cathedral and is not used as living space. In a home with such a shape, the rooms in the upper portions can seem cramped and uncomfortable. You may feel as though the walls are closing in on you. An additional difficulty is that you can't hang mirrors or pictures on such walls or place your furniture against them. Even the bathrooms on these floors will seem uncomfortable small. Also, because the shape represents Fire, it is very important that you pay special attention to the balance of the elements. The advantage in such a shape is that the floors will be square which makes it easy for you to Feng Shui them. If the home has two or more floors, make a separate floor plan and a separate Bagua Map for each floor.

L-shaped – This shape is like two rectangles that have been put together. Both the rectangles will be narrow and shouldn't be confused with a home with missing corners. You need to treat both rectangles as their own separate structures. Place the Bagua separately over each side so that you essentially have two different renditions of the Bagua to balance. One side will be larger than the other, since the elbow of the shape will reside in one side making it the larger side to Feng Shui. It is possible to group the kitchen and living room together, since they are both *yang*. Similarly, you can group the bedrooms and bathrooms together, since they are both *yin*. Let this be your demarcation.

T-shaped – Treat this as two separate homes and make two floor plans. Enhance each plan separately. The other option is to cure the missing corners on both sides of the home.

U-shaped – If this home is very large then it's a good thing to have a U-shaped home. It is believed that the two arms of the U represent the green dragon and the white tiger which embrace the home. If, however, the size of the home is normal, the rules change. If the U is in the front of the house, it means that those who live there are very private. If the U is in the back of the house, its occupants will probably have financial difficulties unless they have a good support system. Regardless, the situation will need to be fixed. To deal with this, take each part of the home as a separate floor plan so that you have three floor plans. Then enhance each one.

Z-shaped – The Z-shaped home can be a rollercoaster of good luck and bad luck. If it isn't possible to make any additions to it, treat it as two separate floor plans and enhance and balance each side of the Feng Shui map separately.

Missing or Projecting Corners and Extensions

Once you've made the floor plans and the Feng Shu Bagua Map, you need to check for missing or projecting corners and extensions. If these are present, the disruption they cause can create chaos in your life. When there is an architectural indent in the floor plan of your structure, you will not be able to apply all of the nine sections of the Bagua to your space.

For example, let's say that the love and relationship corner is missing. In such a case you could be experiencing unfulfilled relationships with the people in your life or even a lack of relationships. The energy field that is missing will bring a lack in your personal or professional life.

Now that you know how to place your Feng Shui maps on differently shaped homes, let's take a look at how to deal with the missing corners or extensions in the irregularly shaped homes.

Missing Corners

A Feng Shui Bagua Map would look something like this image if there are missing corners. This is due to the architecture of the building.

1/3 or More Missing...... (Missing Corners)

This graph shows only one missing section. However, there may be more than one section that is missing and it may happen in a variety of combinations. The shape of your home could be Z-shaped, L-shaped, U-shaped or T-shaped or a combination of two or more of these. The first thing you need to determine is whether what you're looking at is a missing corner or an extension.

When a corner is MISSING, it means that one third or more of the length of the exterior is missing. By the same token, when there is an EXTENSION, less than one third of the length of the exterior is missing.

Extensions

Architectural enhancements, designed to make the house look attractive, such as a porch, patio, a deck or even a bay window, are generally considered extensions.

Remember, when to determine whether a particular portion is an extension, you must check to see whether it is less than one third of the length of the exterior. Similarly, when to determine whether a corner is MISSING, check to see whether it is one third or more than the length of the exterior.

Black Hat Feng Shui considers extensions good luck. The good energy that is created when you enhance your home as per the Bagua Map is extended.

How to Deal with Missing Corners and Extensions

Square Off a Missing Corner from the Exterior

Once it is obvious that there is a missing corner in your Feng Shui Bagua Map, you need to determine whether the corner in question can be squared off from the outside of the building.

You can do many things to square off the missing corner on the outside. The main point is that something must be added where the hypothetical walls of the missing corner would meet.

Some of the things you can use to square off a missing corner are:

- A tree
- One or more bushes
- Landscaping that squares off the corner
- Potted plants
- A fence
- Statues
- Fountain or small pond to enliven the area
- You can also tile the area
- A covered patio
- A flag pole
- A wind chime where the two imaginary walls would have met
- Rocks or boulders strategically place. The bigger they are, the better.
- You can string up lights or lanterns along the two missing sides
- You can install lights higher up the wall so they point down into the area or you can install small decorator lights on the ground.
- Enclose the area

Be creative but economical while coming up the perfect solution to the problem of a missing corner. Regardless of what method you eventually decide to go with to close off the missing corner, make sure that the area is squared off properly. The actual squaring off may not always be possible but stick to your intention of squaring the area off. Keep in mind that intentions are paramount in Feng Shui.

Even though a corner may be missing, it is still a section of your Bagua Map and more importantly, it is related to some part of your life. It is necessary, therefore, to enhance the required element in the corner and balance it as you would do in any other section of the Feng Shui Bagua Map.

Square Off a Missing Corner from the Interior

If you find that you cannot square off the missing corner of the Feng Shui Bagua Map from the exterior of the house, you will need to do so from the interior. You need to enhance the walls that border the missing corner using symbols that make your intention of squaring off the corner clear. Here are some ways that you can square off a missing corner from the interior of your home:

- You can place mirrors on both interior walls to 'expand' the area
- Hang wind chimes
- Place
- potted plants along the length of each wall
- Crystals, especially when there is a window, hung on a 9 inch long red string
- Anything else you can come up with that will enhance the energy there

Remember that the corner missing in your house is also a section missing from your Feng Shui Bagua Map. You need to ensure that the proper element of this missing corner is balanced so that the corresponding aspect of your life is in balance and enhanced too.

You need to add the element as close to the missing corner as possible. The element could be something that you hang on the wall so that it is close to the missing corner or even on the floor close by. For instance, if the missing corner requires the element Metal, then you could place something made of it, such as a metal lamp.

Interior Projecting Corners

If your home has a sharp corner that projects inward into the house, it is the equivalent of having sharp arrows pointed at you. You need to soften the sharpness so destructive energy doesn't enter your body. This type of energy is also referred to as poisoned arrows and "*sha*" or sharp energy.

Remember that energy or '*chi*' is always moving. It can move very slowly, which you don't want or it can move too quickly, which you don't want either. You need the energy to flow in a slow, meandering movement. The problem with a projecting corner is that when energy flows off the sharp corner, it moves too fast. Therefore, the motion it mimics is that of a piercing arrow.

If one is constantly in the way of this sharp energy it can slowly but surely begin to manifest as an irritable disposition. For instance, if every night as you lay in bed, work at your desk, or watch television each night, the sharp energy enters your body. This energy can make you feel miserable and impact your ability to get the best out of your life. It can also cause problems for all members of the household since one person's bad mood affects everyone.

If a person's energy level is compromised, or sickness or disease is already present in the body, then the effects of long term projecting sharp energy could be even more debilitating.

You can find a projecting, sharp corner in any part of your home. Many different architectural enhancements can create sharp corners. A fireplace mantel with sharp edges, pillars that are squared or a wall that is built out in the form of a sharp corner is an example of a projecting, sharp corner.

If the corner is rounded, it doesn't pose a problem. The problem happens when the corner is pointed. Look around your home. There are probably some sharp corners that you have never taken notice of. Be sure not to sit for long in a place where a sharp corner points straight in your direction.

Here are some ways to balance out this "cutting" energy:

- Large plants in front of the sharp corner
- Wind chimes hung in front of the corner to break up the sharp energy
- A large round faceted crystal hung from the ceiling in front of the sharp corner
- A decorative screen to hide the sharp corner
- You can change the shape of the corner to a more rounded one by plastering it.

It is extremely important that you identify and deal with missing or projecting sharp corners when you balance your home using the Feng Shui Bagua Map. Without this balance, the issues you could face could hold you back with respect to your health, finances, relationships, creativity, career, education, happiness, and choices in life and how people view you and what they think of you.

As your consciousness evolves, your understanding of Feng Shui will evolve with you. You will probably want to stretch out and make even more positive improvements to the Feng Shui work that you have already done.

Chapter 5: The Significance of Each Feng Shui Color

Colors are significant in Feng Shui just as arrangement is. Different colors emit individual energy forces that can decrease or increase your success in certain areas of your life. When these colors are used indiscriminately, they tend to disrupt the good effects of Feng Shui.

The colors of Feng Shui are extremely powerful and can change the energy in a room instantly. The Feng Shui or atmosphere which is created can either build or destroy your vitality and thinking. We'll discuss how you can use the correct colors in the correct manner so that you can ensure that you're building positive energy, clarity, and happiness. This is as opposed to sluggishness and negative habitual emotions that far too many people deal with unsuccessfully, all because of bad Feng Shui. We'll talk about which colors are best for each room in your house, and where on the Feng Shui Bagua Map they are.

Color is vibration. As per Feng Shui, everything around us lives, is made up of energy and has a specific frequency that it vibrates at. The same is true for Feng Shui colors — each color vibrates at its own unique frequency. Just as you and your home are connected through a multitude of overlapping energy fields, you are connected to the colors in your home.

Your inner reality and your outer reality are separated by your home which acts as a doorway between them. Your home is a reflection of who you are in this moment and can also be used as a tool to determine your direction for the future. Therefore, you need to use color psychology in conjunction with Feng Shui to create your direction and your reality. Your physiology and psychology can be deeply impacted by color. An understanding of the colors used in Feng Shui can help you bring about positive changes in your life. Do remember that everything is connected and made of energy. So, when you change the energy in your home, it directly affects you. The effects can be very substantial, and far too often explain why people are unhappy and lethargic.

There is no one specific way to use colors in your home. Therefore, here are a few guidelines to keep in mind when you use Feng Shui colors.

- Think about what the common effects of color on psychology are and see what colors work for you.
- Go through the different sections of the Feng Shui Bagua Map and determine what colors are associated with each aspect mentioned therein.
- Find out what colors are suitable for which rooms as per the principles of Feng Shui.

Follow your instincts but also your judgment. Use colors that you enjoy and which don't leave you feeling enervated but instead make you energetic. For example, if you are told that red is a powerful color but you hate it, don't use it. Instead pick a color that makes you think of power. In the end it's all about your intentions and everyone is too different for the colors to mean the same thing to everyone.

Feng Shui Colors: What Do They Mean and Where Can They Be Used

Orange

As per psychology, orange is cheerful. It is also supposed to be pleasantly stimulating, sociable and active. It represents the fire element. You can use orange in the interior of your house in the fame/reputation of the Bagua. It can also be used in the love/relationship and prosperity/abundance area.

Rooms you should use this color are the dining room, living room and kitchen – all three rooms are social rooms and the color is sociable. If you plan to use it in the bedroom, make sure it is an earthy orange.

Purple

There is a reason that royalty wore purple. It is supposed to mean dignity, nobility and abundance. The color can be calm and soothing and is connected to spirituality. If you want to enhance the prosperity/abundance area of the Bagua, use purple – it's the most appropriate.

If you want to Feng Shui your bedroom in the color, use shades such as violet and lavender to make the room more romantic.

Grey

Grey is a color devoid of energy; it is quiet and calm, almost neutral. The color can make you feel bored and drained. It is a very conservative color. Grey is used to represent the Metal element. It is best used in the helpful people/travel, skills/knowledge and creativity/children aspect of the Bagua.

It is not a good idea to paint your walls grey. Instead use it to paint or decorate accessories.

Brown

Brown is a down-to-earth, stable, reliable, comfortable and even maternal color. In the practice of Feng Shui, brown is linked to two elements – wood and water. You can use it in the skills/knowledge aspect of the Bagua.

Brown is best used in the living room and bedroom.

Red

As per color psychology, red is exciting, stimulating and powerful. Red is the color of the Fire element in Feng Shui. It denotes love, passion, romance and luxury. It only follows then that red be used in the abundance/prosperity, relationships/love and fame/reputation aspects of the Bagua.

The kitchen, living room and dining room can be painted in or decorated with red. If you're planning to use it in the bedroom pick a more earthy shade of the color.

Yellow

In color psychology, yellow is a happy color also denoting warmth, upliftment, expansiveness and stimulation. It too is a Fire element color and is best used in the fame/reputation aspect along with the relationship/love and abundance/prosperity aspects of the Bagua.

It can be used in the living room, dining room and kitchen. In the bedroom more earthy or pale shades of yellow should be used.

Green

Green has a very calming effect on our psyches. In addition it is said to be relaxing, healing, tranquil and balancing. The color represents the Wood element in Feng Shui. It is best used in the skill/knowledge, health and family/elders sections of the Bagua.

Greens are best used in the bathroom.

Blue

Blue, in color psychology is soothing, relaxing and healing. It also means trustworthiness, reliability and security. Blue represents the Water element in Feng Shui and is best used in the abundance/prosperity, career/journey and skills/knowledge sections of the Bagua.

Blue is one of the best Feng Shui colors that can be used in the bathroom.

Black

Black is sophistication, modernity, elegance and power. It also means mystery. It represents the Water element. It should be used in the skill/knowledge, helpful people/travel and career/journey aspects.

Black is best used as an accessory color.

White

White has long meant purity and innocence. It also means hope, clarity and spirituality. It represents the Metal element. As such, it should be used in the helpful people/travel and creativity/children aspects of the Bagua.

Since white is a symbol of purity and cleanliness, it can be used in the bathroom.

Pink

Pink calms and sedates. It also represents romance and love in Feng Shui, making it perfect for the relationships/love area of the Bagua.

Thanks to its connotations, it is an ideal color for the bedroom.

Here's a more detailed list of the colors mentioned previously, so you can be sure to use the correct ones.

- **Wealth, Money, and Financial Abundance (Southeast)** – brown, green, gold and purple

- **Reputation, Fame, and Celebrity (South)** – red

- **Love, Romance, Marriage, and Partnership (Southwest)** – earth colors: pinks, light yellow, light brown, cream, beige

- **Inspiration, Creativity, Ingenuity, Children, and Joy (West)** - white and gray

- **Travel, Friendships, Helpful People, and Blessings (Northwest)** – white, gray and pastel

- **Family Bonds, and New Beginnings (East)** – brown and green

- **Life Journey and Career Path (North)** – black and blue

- **Wisdom, Self-Awareness, and Spiritual Growth (Northeast)** – earthly colors such as, light yellow, cream, beige, and some blues

- **Wellbeing, Unity, Physical Health, Stability, and Balance (Center)** – earthly colors such as yellow, tan and brown.

For the Compass Bagua Map, the center space is empty because it's where the energy force is balanced and stabilized, meanwhile for the Form Bagua Map, the center area represents health. This is because if you don't have balance in the energy fields in your body, your mental, spiritual, and physical health suffers.

Enhance your home with the colors indicated for each area and enjoy the benefits of using Feng Shui.

Chapter 6: Benefits of Feng Shui

There are countless benefits of Feng Shui that you can enjoy once you have learned how to maximize its use. All the facets indicated in your Bagua Map will improve to support the realization of your goals. This list includes the spiritual, mental, social, and physical advantages you can gain from good Feng Shui practices.

1. Enhances positive energy

Positive energy is enhanced and increased wherever you used Feng Shui correctly. It doesn't matter whether you used it in your home, office, or wherever. The positive energy will always increase in that area, providing you with the ability to improve and enhance your positive traits.

Your spiritual growth is also promoted by this positive energy. You grow more in kindness and love for other people. You learn how to cultivate your positive traits towards helping other people.

2. Provides the power of self-direction

When all the energy fields in your home are harmonized, this will provide you the power to re-direct your life the way you want to. This is due to the fact that you now have sufficient Chi (total energy) to do so.

3. Promotes good health

Because Feng Shui maintains balance in the body, it promotes good health. Once you've enriched all the different aspects in the Feng Shui Map or square, your whole life will change for the better. Also, the Yin and Yang will be balanced appropriately, allowing you to maintain mental, social, spiritual, and physical health.

4. Boosts chances of success in career

When you enrich the Feng Shui space that corresponds to your career, your chances of success are increased tremendously. The energy coming from that area will provide you with a power boost that will catapult you towards the path of triumph.

5. Improves relationships

Due to the positive, constructive energy field existing in your home, your relationships with family members, friends, and loved ones will improve because you'll be less irritable, indifferent, and grumpy. You'll be more amiable, calm, and happy. Everyone loves happy and jovial people.

6. Increases chances of success at home

As your relationships are fortified, your home will become happier and more peaceful. Likewise, there will be unity and cooperation among family members to achieve a more peaceful home environment.

7. Hones creativity

You become more ingenious. You will acquire the power of thinking out of the box, which will benefit your career. If you're a writer, you'll be able to catch your muse easily. You'll effortlessly have eureka moments in which new ideas manifest themselves in your consciousness to promote your undertakings or your business.

8. Provides energy for success in money matters

Feng Shui provides potent energy to help you prosper with money matters. You may not be able to see this energy but it's there once you comply with the requirements of the Feng Shui Bagua Map and its enhancements. In Feng Shui, your kitchen area is closely related to money matters, therefore, ensure that it's spic and span, and every appliance is in good working order.

9. Boosts mental acuity

It boosts your ability to acquire knowledge and sharpens your mental skills and cognitive abilities. This is a result of the ever-flowing positive energy all over your body which flows freely back and forth from your heart, brain, and circulatory system.

10. Allows you a healthy, peaceful, and meaningful existence

Feng Shui will allow you to live a meaningful, peaceful, and healthy existence through its empowering and revitalizing energy in all aspects of your life.

These are only some of the major benefits you can obtain from the practice of Feng Shui. There are sure to be more advantages that you'll discover as you practice this incredible science of spaces and energy.

Chapter 7: Additional Useful Tools in Feng Shui

There are some guides or tools in the practice of Feng Shui that you can use to ensure that your Feng Shui will be effective and done correctly.

1. **Kua (Pa Kua or Gua – from Bagua) numbers or Feng Shui numbers**

   This is an important tool for Feng Shui to determine the auspicious areas where you can succeed. It also identifies the area in which people are categorized. These are numbers assigned to you based on your year of birth and gender. It's commonly computed by adding the last two digits of your birth year, and then adding them again until they become one whole number.

   ### Calculating Kua numbers for a male

   An example is if you were born in the year 2014, you get the last two digits, which is 14 and add them to get a whole number; 1+4 =

5. If the answer is still two digits, you have to add them again until you get a whole number (for example: 1988 → 8+8=16, then 1+6=7). Subtract the result from 10 to obtain your Kua numbers. In the first example, you subtract 5 from 10. Hence, 10-5 = 5, which is your Kua number.

Calculating Kua numbers for a female

You do the same computations but instead of subtracting from 10, you add 5 to your result. An example is when your year of birth is 1956; you add 5+6 = 11; then 1+1 = 2. Add 5 to your answer; 2+5 = 7. Hence, your Kua number is 7.

If you were born before February 4, use the year before the year of your birth. An example is if you were born in January 1971, then use the year 1970 to compute your Kua numbers.

Determine your lucky areas/corners in the Feng Shui chart using your Kua number. Each number has an auspicious corner among the 9 squares or grids based on the square

Bagua Map. This refers to the three major areas namely, love (L), health (H), and success (S), respectively. The location of the number in your compass Bagua Map is also indicated.

- **One (1)** – south (L), east (H), and southeast (S)

- **Two (2)** – south (L), east (H), and southeast (S)

- **Three (3)** – southeast (L), south (H), north (S)

- **Four (4)** – east (L), north (H), south (S)

- **Five (5)** – for men: northwest (L), northeast (H), west (S)

  For women: west (L), southwest (H), northwest (S)

- **Six (6)** – southwest (L), west (H), northeast (S)

- **Seven (7)** – northeast (L), northwest (H), southwest (S)

- **Eight (8)** – west (L), southwest (H), northwest (S)

○ **Nine (9)** – north (L), east (H), south (S)

You can also refer to the Feng Shui chart or Lo Shu square, where the first row of upper boxes correspond to numbers 4, 9, and 2, from left to right. The second row of squares from left to right belong to numbers 3, 5, and 7. The last row and bottom three squares are designated for numbers 8, 1, and 6.

Interpret your Kua number using the Feng Shui Bagua chart or the Lo Shu Square and know your lucky areas or corners. This can help you determine your traits. If your Kua number is 7, for you to succeed in love, you must choose the northeast position; in health – the northwest corner; and for success – the southwest square. The element for square 7 is metal. This means that you have a propensity to travel and an interest in creativity and the arts, as indicated in your Bagua Map.

The method mentioned can often be confusing, but never fear, you can also interpret it easily through these groupings:

West group Kua numbers = 2, 5, 6, 7, 8

East group Kua numbers = 1, 3, 4, 9

These groupings mean that if your number belongs to the East group, then the best position for you is facing the east or southeast, south and north. If your number belongs to the West group then the ideal position is for you to face the west or northwest and southwest.

2. Lo-Shu Magic Square

This is actually your Feng Shui Bagua Map but serves a different purpose. You can use this chart to determine your personality and that of another person. Take note of the colors and numbers and you can superimpose this with your previous Bagua Map from Chapter 4.

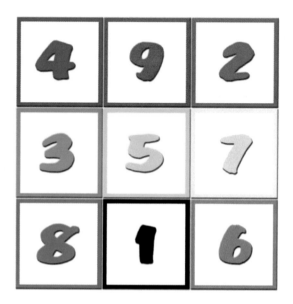

This square is also called the "Nine-Star Ki" because each number corresponds to a star in the galaxy.

All these are additional tools you can use in your Feng Shui. You can adapt these tools to attain success in your Feng Shui practice.

Remember, though, that you have to eliminate all negative thoughts in your mind and welcome positive thoughts for Feng Shui to succeed.

The expected traits based on your Feng Shui squares are the following:

- **One (1)** – Your element is water so you are most likely interested in writing. You're also amiable, diplomatic, and can become a good leader.

- **Two (2)** – Your element is earth. You tend to nurture people around you. You can succeed as a teacher and in careers that require diplomacy, fairness, and helpfulness.

- **Three (3)** – Your element is wood. You're ambitious in a positive way, a good leader, and an outspoken person. You can succeed in life as an actor or a politician.

- **Four (4)** – Your element is the same as Kua number 3 – wood. This indicates that you're flexible and trustworthy. You will most likely become an actor, a politician, or a singer.

- **Five (5)** – Your element is earth, which is the center of the Bagua Map. You have the ability to inspire other people. Since your number is found at the center, your personality draws on all the other squares.

- o **Six (6)** – Your element is metal. You have a propensity towards the invention of new things. You're authoritative and can be a superb leader. However, your attempts at perfection can stymie your efforts for success.

- o **Seven (7)** – Your element is metal. You tend to be optimistic, charming, and jovial. Your interest lies in the arts and entertainment. You can become a good actor, writer, and performer.

- o **Eight (8)** – Your element is earth. You have a strong personality. You're the silent type who can be good at learning and studying, and would be good at being a philosopher.

- o **Nine (9)** – Your element is fire. You're a risk-taker, who is passionate in pursuing his goals. You communicate well with other people, and you have the ability to lead and initiate changes in your community. You can engage in a career that requires you to be a major proponent of change.

Your personal Feng Shui number (Kua number) can reveal a number of things about you, so compute your precious Kua number and remember it.

Refer to these tools in your Feng Shui practice and you'll experience more success in the various facets of your life.

Chapter 8: Other Important Feng Shui Tips

Aside from knowing about the how to use the Feng Shui Bagua Map and how to interpret your Kua numbers, you should also use these tips to acquaint you more with Feng Shui.

1. **Eschew all negative thoughts, emotions, and ideas**. You can only succeed in Feng Shui if you throw away all your negative thoughts. Take note that Feng Shui is harnessing your energy through positive thoughts.

2. **Observe the Golden Rule.** Do to others what you want them to do to you. Karma is an inevitable law of nature. What you give is what you'll receive. This is one principle that you should practice together with Feng Shui.

3. **Practicing Feng Shui is a lifetime process.** For you to become truly successful in all aspects of your life, you have to practice Feng Shui for life. It won't be effective if you do it once and then stop. De-cluttering and

maintaining your Feng Shui spaces should be a lifelong process.

4. **Use Feng Shui to change for the better.** There should be not only external change in your home, but also an internal change in you and your attitude. If you welcome Feng Shui wholeheartedly, then this won't be a problem.

5. **Bagua extensions amplify the energy.** If there are extensions of your house outside of the Bagua Map, don't worry, because this extension will boost the energy of that particular area.

6. **Feng Shui can be utilized for specific rooms in your home.** You can also use Feng Shui in your office, or in any location that you want.

7. **Live a healthy life.** Even if you use Feng Shui to enhance your energy for health, if you counter this with your unhealthy lifestyle, then Feng Shui won't be as effective as it should be. Feng Shui will eliminate trash or toxic substances from your body, but if you keep

acquiring trash and toxic substances from drugs, cigarettes, and alcohol, then the process will just be a cycle of unending elimination and acquisition. In this case, stability cannot be maintained.

8. **There is such a thing as bad Feng Shui.** Bad Feng Shui is when the energies existing around you are in conflict with one another; your home is cluttered, furniture is arranged haphazardly, and your Bagua Map is not followed. So beware of bad Feng Shui; it represents bad luck, which will be detrimental to your success.

9. **Use your Feng Shui knowledge intelligently.** Be an intelligent user by accomplishing things correctly through your Feng Shui knowledge. If you're not careful, you might accomplish the opposite and disrupt the Chi in your environment.

10. **Apply Feng Shui to each of the rooms in your house.** This is ideal because each corner or area in your house must be attuned to the other energy fields/forces existing around you.

11. **De-clutter every room regularly.** You can only allow Feng Shui to work when the areas are de-cluttered. Any room in your environment that is cluttered is an obstacle for good Feng Shui, so de-clutter regularly to prevent accumulation of bad energy.

12. **Use the five elements generously in their indicated areas.** Display the element as much as you can in their designated areas but don't clutter the area. Otherwise, you'll disrupt the smooth flow of energy.

13. **Remember to use colors for good Feng Shui.** Besides arrangement and positioning, colors also play a crucial role in good Feng Shui, so use them optimally.

14. **Define your goals clearly.** Well-defined goals will facilitate your success, so design your goals clearly by being more specific. Instead of stating: "I'll be successful in my career in 2015," say instead: "I'll be the CEO of my company in January 2015."

15. Share your knowledge of good Feng Shui with other people. Share your good fortune with other people by sharing your positive experience with Feng Shui. Sharing doubles your gains, and good karma is just around the corner.

These are all essential tips that you should remember when practicing Feng Shui. Neglecting any of them can result in bad Feng Shui and bad luck.

In addition, there are some tips that you can use to enhance the energy flow in your home.

- **Fix Squeaks in Your Front Door**

The front door is the first thing you come across when entering your home and the last thing while leaving it. If it squeaks or makes a whining sound when you use it, your disposition and even your health can be adversely affected. You may have gotten used to the sound to the point that you don't even notice it, but it will still affect you. Make sure to oil the hinges periodically to eliminate any squeaks. Do this not only for your front door but also other doors and windows in the house.

- **Use Your Front Door**

You may have a house in which you drive into the garage and use a connecting door, most often the back door, to enter your home. Although you may find it more convenient this way, Feng Shui states that this limits the positive energy and thus good opportunities in your life. '*Chi*' uses the front door to enter your home and therefore, your life so use the front door at least a few times a week – the more, the better. For example, when you go to collect your mail or go out for a walk, use the front door. Make it a part of your regular routine.

- **Place the Feng Shui Fountain Appropriately**

One of the meanings of Water in Feng Shui is wealth. You may want to know what the best place is to install a Feng Shui fountain. Feng Shui states that one of the best places for the

Water element is near the entry or the front door of your home. You can place it just outside the front door or just inside, depending upon the space you have. What is most important is that the water in the fountain shouldn't flow inwards but outwards in the direction of the center of your house. This allows wealth to come into your life.

- **Kitchen Cabinets and Plants**

If your kitchen cabinets are built up to a soffit or the ceiling of your home, it is considered good Feng Shui. There shouldn't be any space above the kitchen cabinets. This is because this space becomes a home for stagnant or dead energy and, of course, dust. This dead energy may prevent you from moving forward in life. However, all is not lost. Feng Shui offers a solution, if there is a space. Bring life into the area by putting plants, lighting or well-loved and attractive objects. Soon you will feel the dead energy being transformed into life.

- **Close the Bathroom Door**

When enhancing their homes with Feng Shui, many people get worried about the bathroom. The bathroom is the room where water goes out of the house and in large quantities too. Since the Water element is supposed to be associated with wealth, it may seem as though your wealth is being flushed away. Of course, as a tank empties, it also fills up, but there is no need to take chances. It is best to keep the toilet seat cover down and the door of the bathroom closed to minimize the effect of the water flowing away.

- **Location of Your Bed**

Feng Shui uses the 'commanding' principle when it comes to deciding where to place important pieces of furniture such as your bed. In fact, your bed is the most important furnishing to be located as per the commanding position. After all, you do spend a significant portion of your life sleeping in it. Here's how to locate the bed in the commanding position. Place the bed facing the door but not so you'd be in line with the door while lying in it. One option is to put it diagonally across the room from the door. This, however, may not always be possible. As an alternative, you can use a mirror, whether on the wall or a freestanding one. Place it in such a position that while you're lying in the bed, the door is visible.

- **Don't Leave the TV in the Bedroom Uncovered**

Since we tend to use the bedroom to relax, we often have our TVs in there. If you have trouble getting to sleep, experience broken sleep or even if you sleep soundly, when not using the TV, keep it covered. The active energy emanated by the television can be disruptive to the peace and quiet you need to have in a bedroom so you can sleep undisturbed. Get a TV cover or just use a pretty piece of cloth to cover it.

- **Clean the Windows**

Just because spring cleaning is several months away doesn't mean that the dirt and grime on the window should be allowed to accumulate and crust up. The windows are like the eyes of the house, therefore your eyes, looking out on the world. With dirty windows you are effectively blinded to everything the universe offers you. So pick up an old newspaper, collect a bottle of cleaning spray or better yet a solution of water and vinegar and start scrubbing. Come into the light.

- **Make the Front Path or Porch Colorful and Fragrant**

Pathways offer opportunities a route to find their way to us. You can make these pathways inviting by planting pretty and colorful flowers and plants along them. Such an act also suggests that you enjoy good health – after all, gardening is a healthy way to exercise.

- **Hang a Wind Chime Outside the Front Door**

A Feng Shui wind chime often comes with spiral rods. These rods can attract and direct very good energy into your life. Also as it releases its musical notes, a wind chime attracts attention, making more good energy wend its way into your space.

- **Make Sure Your Address Is Visible**

Make sure your address can be seen clearly. If it is old and faded, paint it again. If numbers are loose or have fallen off, tighten them or replace them. Make sure that your name is posted properly and correctly if you live in an apartment building.

- **Fix the Floor**

Check if any tile or an area of flooring is broken. If you find that a part of the floor is broken in your home, get it repaired or replaced, as soon as possible, because the negative energy it spreads may affect your relationship with your family members. If repairing it is not possible, you may also put a carpet to cover the damaged area.

- **Fish and Water**

Flowing water and floating fish are considered very auspicious in Feng Shui. They invite in positive energy and get rid of negative energy. Don't go overboard and ensure that you do what you need to do correctly. If you're planning to install a water feature, pick a smaller size and make sure that the water is clean and it flows. If you have a fish tank/aquarium, clean it regularly and refresh the water in it frequently. A small statue of fish placed in your bedroom or elsewhere in your house can help prevent bad luck.

- **Placement**

Locate your bed in such a manner that you don't face a mirror. In other words, you shouldn't be able to see your reflection in a mirror while lying in your bed. In the kitchen, the stove and sink should not be directly opposite to each other. Doors and gates into your home should open inwards and should be two leaf doors so that the good *Qi* is invited into your home. You can use a tall gate in the West to create an obstacle for negative *yang* energy. Hanging a wind chime over your bed is not a good idea since it absorbs negative energy and may release it while you are sleeping. Try to make sure that there is no tree in direct line with your front door or main window. This could end up in your family member's suffering from ill health. If there is such a tree, place a convex mirror on the wall facing the tree.

- **Good Outside Feng Shui**

A home with good Feng Shui has no negative energy such as *sha chi* or *si chi* surrounding it. Houses located in a cul de sac, close to the railroad, T-junction homes, or those with a sloping backyard can attract negative energy and will need to be taken care of.

- **Strong Feng Shui Trinity**

The main rooms of the house, the bathroom, bedroom and kitchen are the centers where good Feng Shui is anchored. Therefore, the quality of Feng Shui in your house is determined by the quality of the energy in these three rooms. Make sure that the rooms have been enhanced and keep an eye on the energy in these rooms.

There can be no good Feng Shui house without a good Feng Shui bedroom, a good Feng Shui kitchen and a good Feng Shui bathroom.

- **Fresh Feng Shui Energy**

A home with good Feng Shui has no dead, old, stagnant or blocked energy in it. Instead, it is characterized by freely flowing, fresh and clear energy. Since everything is always in a state of flux, don't just stop once you've created a good Feng Shui foundation. Keep working to ensure that the energy continues to flow freely and clearly and keep a watch out for areas where energy can stagnate.

- **Solid House Backing**

As mentioned earlier, a house that has a sloped backyard can be considered a Feng

Shui challenge. This is because a sloped backyard means that the house has no supporting energy as it flows away down the slope. As per Feng Shui tradition, the back of the house is considered the area of the tortoise, one of the five celestial Feng Shui animals. The tortoise's energy is believed to help with supporting and stabilizing the house.

Ancient masters of Feng Shui compared a house to a human body in terms of its complex functions. Think about it like this. When you have good lumbar support, for example, a comfortable armchair, your body is comfortable. Similarly, so that good Feng Shui energy can be created and used to maintain good energy for the occupants of the house, it needs solid backing.

If there is stagnant or old energy in your house in a specific area, it will soon make itself felt in the corresponding aspect of your life in the Feng Shui Bagua Map.

Smart Feng Shui Garden Design

A proper garden design as per Feng Shui guidelines attracts very good Feng Shui energy into your home. It's not too hard on the eyes either.

A good Feng Shui design does not mean a large garden. A large garden is an added advantage but even without it you can still create a great Feng Shui garden.

The Bagua map is the tool you need to create a good Feng Shui garden. You can't do this independently of your house. You need to know the Bagua of your house to be able to create a good Feng Shui garden.

Clear Spaces

Last but not least, do a space clearing. Your house and surroundings take in and keep the energy that is released by those who live there. Take out a little time to get rid of the old energy and welcome new and fresh 'chi' in to your home. There are many ways to do a cleansing – you can spray natural orange oils mixed with water around the house, you can burn palo santo or you can smudge the house using white sage. The orange oil works to improve your mood, the palo santo is light and can therefore, be used everyday and the white sage is useful when you want to do a thorough and proper cleansing. No matter which of these methods you decide upon ensure that while performing the act you keep imagining that your house is being filled with good and positive energy and that your dreams and ambitions are being fulfilled. In Feng Shui, intention is what counts.

Chapter 9: Myths About Feng Shui

Since its adoption by the West, Feng Shui has become the subject of many myths and misconceptions. It does not help that there are many schools of thought in Feng Shui and none of them can be said to be superior to the others. These days every home décor outlet and mall keeps knick-knacks that will supposedly Feng Shui your home. You also have practitioners of Feng Shui coming out of the woodwork the moment you decide to get a consultant for Feng Shui. Therefore, to avoid the pitfalls of getting bad Feng Shui, here are some myths and misconceptions that you need to keep in mind.

Feng Shui of Lucky Red Color Front Door

It is a myth that a door colored red is lucky in terms of Feng Shui. It may be, but that's not true of every house. The use of color in Feng Shui is not so simplistic. In fact, it is quite specific and must be used depending on various factors. If you want to know what color to paint your door, you need to keep in mind what direction it faces.

Lucky Bamboo and Fountains

The most popular accessories in Feng Shui are the indoor fountains and the lucky bamboo plant. Many people believe that all they have to do to have good Feng Shui is install one or the other or both in the house. While these items are efficient cures in Feng Shui, whether at home or in office, that doesn't mean that if you don't have them you have bad Feng Shui. Similarly, their presence doesn't automatically signify good Feng Shui either. Feng Shui involves a lot more than just buying a few items and setting them up in your home.

It's a good start, though.

Flowers Are Bad Bedroom Feng Shui

This is a very common misconception. Flowers actually have very good *chi* and bring a sense of healing and fresh fragrance to their surroundings. It doesn't follow, therefore, that they are bad Feng Shui for the bedroom. There are no one size fits all principles in Feng Shui. Everything has to be taken in conjunction with other conditions. A small bouquet is perfect for your bedroom. A large bouquet might bring in too much color and energy into a room that is meant to be restful.

Move Your Furniture, Change Your Life

Well, this one sounds like a super quick fix. Move your couch and get promoted. Do you really think Feng Shui is as easy and uncomplicated as that? While rearranging your furniture from time to time to refresh and redirect the flow of energy is always a good idea, it is no guarantee of a major change in your life. To create changes that last, you need to do a lot more than just change the positions of a few pieces of furniture.

If Your Bed Is Not Facing a Lucky Direction, You Are Doomed

The doom and ill luck misconceptions are as popular as the quick fixes in Feng Shui. The one used to scare people the most is that if the position of your bed is such that it faces a direction considered unlucky, you will face all manner of misfortune. Trust me when I say – no, this is not true.

The Right Plant Brings Luck and Money

Who doesn't want wealth quickly and easily? Feng Shui tradition has plenty of money plants or plants that bring in wealth. You can check them all out and determine which one you want to bring in. However, any healthy and vibrant plant which has soft and flowing energy can bring you a lot of good energy because it is part of nature and nature is the origin of all abundance. This means that instead of spending a lot of money and time looking for that perfect Feng Shui money plant, you are much better off taking care of the plants you do have. A money plant isn't going to do you much good if the existing plants in your home are sickly or dying. That is just a surefire way to attract negative energy.

The Stove Direction Makes Your Kitchen

The kitchen can be the heart of the house. All the family's health and wellness flow from there. A lot of factors go into making a kitchen that works well and looks good. Feng Shui is no different. In Feng Shui too there are a lot of considerations that determine whether your kitchen has good energy. The direction of the kitchen stove is nowhere near the top of that list. Instead of worrying about positioning the stove in the right direction, concentrate on creating a healthy, clean and bright space that speaks to your family's happiness.

Mandarin Ducks Bring Everlasting Love

Anyone searching for true and everlasting love has heard of this one and perhaps even fallen for it. Mandarin ducks are supposed to ensure that your marriage is happy and that your partner is loving and devoted. Guess what? Yes, that's right. This one's a myth too. Your relationship is as complicated as any Feng Shui process. You need to work on it along with your partner. If you're contentious and selfish, no Mandarin duck is going to make your partner devoted.

Displaying Clocks Is Bad Feng Shui

No this rule isn't that simple. Time is non-renewable and slips out of our hands. Clocks keep track of time. Therefore, you do need to be careful about displaying big clocks just anywhere in the house, only because they give you unnecessary reminders of time flowing out of your hands. Don't display the big clock in your bedroom since the reminder is hardly conducive to a restful area but you can display as many clocks as you want elsewhere.

A Bagua Mirror Will Protect Your Home

Yes it will, but it depends upon how you use it. Many people use it liberally in the house believing that it is good Feng Shui. Actually a Bagua mirror is a defense mechanism. Regardless of whether it is concave or convex, a Bagua mirror is only meant for the outside of your home, never for the inside. Even on the outside, it should be used if and only if *sha chi* or attacking energy is pointing at your front door. In fact, it is best to use something else to protect your home rather than a mirror which is going to look really strange to your neighbors.

Feng Shui Chachkis Are Good for Your Home

Chachkis or ornaments such as fu dogs, toads with coins inside, paintings and even purple pillows do nothing to alter the energy in your home. These are representations of harmony, wealth and protection in the East. In the West, for some reason they've been joined with Feng Shui when in actual fact, they have nothing to do with it.

116

Feng Shui for Cats and Dogs

There is no such thing. Feng Shui takes into account human energy. However, if your home has good Feng Shui you'll certainly see its effects on your animal companions.

Small Crystals Bring Better Feng Shui

In order to truly feel the effects a crystal has, you'd need to get huge crystal geodes that are more than 3 or 4 feet high and place them in strategic positions around your home. The smaller crystals may work in terms of healing but they aren't big enough to make a difference to the energy in an area.

The Five Elements Have to Be in Every Room

Nope. This one's not true and really exhausting to try to execute. Elements in real Feng Shui represent characteristics of how energy behaves. It's not meant to be literal.

Bamboo Flutes Are Great in Terms of Feng Shui

They're bamboo. It sounds good in theory, since bamboo is strong, that it can create strength and support. However, no one has ever truly gained anything from their use.

Conclusion

Feng Shui is a powerful tool for harmonizing energy fields around you. You can harness this power to improve your home, career, and your personal life. You'll have to persevere if things don't go your way at first. Persistence is the key to success. There are instances when change is difficult to achieve. Nevertheless, when you meet the challenge and succeed in turning your environment into a good Feng Shui area, all your efforts will be rewarded generously.

The benefits you'll obtain from Feng Shui are immense and unending. Your health will get better; your career path will be promising, your relationships will be strengthened, and your life will go through the road of happiness, tranquility, and success.

Use the knowledge you've learned about Feng Shui from this book, and get out there and do it. Don't be held back by the notion that it must be absolutely perfect in the first attempt. Feng Shui is something you can continue to tweak over time as you notice things changing in your life. It's better to make one or two small adjustments at a time, then to make none at all.

Finally, I'd like to thank you for purchasing this book! If you enjoyed it or found it helpful, I'd greatly appreciate it if you'd take a moment to leave a review on Amazon. Thank you!

Made in the USA
Columbia, SC
11 July 2023

20261569R00071